D1710106

AWESOME DOGS

Mastiffs

by Paige V. Polinsky

BLASTOFF!
READERS
2

BELLWETHER MEDIA • MINNEAPOLIS, MN

Reader

Note to Librarians, Teachers, and Parents:

Blastoff! Readers are carefully developed by literacy experts and combine standards-based content with developmentally appropriate text.

Level 1 provides the most support through repetition of high-frequency words, light text, predictable sentence patterns, and strong visual support.

Level 2 offers early readers a bit more challenge through varied simple sentences, increased text load, and less repetition of high-frequency words.

Level 3 advances early-fluent readers toward fluency through increased text and concept load, less reliance on visuals, longer sentences, and more literary language.

Level 4 builds reading stamina by providing more text per page, increased use of punctuation, greater variation in sentence patterns, and increasingly challenging vocabulary.

Level 5 encourages children to move from "learning to read" to "reading to learn" by providing even more text, varied writing styles, and less familiar topics.

Whichever book is right for your reader, Blastoff! Readers are the perfect books to build confidence and encourage a love of reading that will last a lifetime!

This edition first published in 2019 by Bellwether Media, Inc.

No part of this publication may be reproduced in whole or in part without written permission of the publisher. For information regarding permission, write to Bellwether Media, Inc., Attention: Permissions Department, 6012 Blue Circle Drive, Minnetonka, MN 55343.

Library of Congress Cataloging-in-Publication Data

Names: Polinsky, Paige V., author.
Title: Mastiffs / by Paige V. Polinsky.
Description: Minneapolis, MN : Bellwether Media, Inc., 2019. | Series: Blastoff! Readers. Awesome Dogs | Audience: Age 5-8. | Audience: Grade K to 3. | Includes bibliographical references and index.
Identifiers: LCCN 2017056571 (print) | LCCN 2018005281 (ebook) | ISBN 9781626177932 (hardcover : alk. paper | ISBN 9781681035321 (ebook)
Subjects: LCSH: Mastiff–Juvenile literature.
Classification: LCC SF429.M36 (ebook) | LCC SF429.M36 P65 2019 (print) | DDC 636.73–dc23
LC record available at https://lccn.loc.gov/2017056571

Editor: Rebecca Sabelko   Designer: Jeffrey Kollock

Printed in the United States of America, North Mankato, MN.

Table of Contents

What Are Mastiffs?

Mastiffs are the heaviest dogs in the world. They can weigh more than 200 pounds (91 kilograms)!

These calm dogs are sometimes called English Mastiffs.

Mastiff Profile

large body

blocky head

floppy cheeks

wide chest

Life Span: 6 to 10 years

Trainability:

1　　2　　3　　4　　5　　6

Hardest to train　　　　　　Easiest to train

Mastiffs have large bodies with wide chests. Floppy cheeks hang from their blocky heads.

Many have **wrinkles** above their eyes.

wrinkles

Coats and Colors

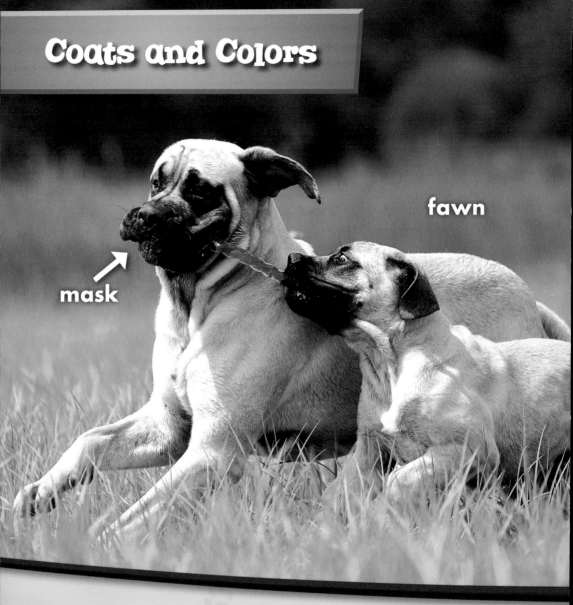

fawn

mask

Mastiffs have short, straight fur.
They can be **fawn** or reddish-tan.
Brindle is also common.

x

8

Mastiff Coats

reddish-tan   brindle

All mastiffs have black **masks**.
Some have white on their chests.

History of Mastiffs

Mastiffs were brought to England around 500 BCE.

England

N
W E
S

10

The **breed** appeared about 5,000 years ago. Many people think the first mastiffs came from Asia. They were very strong.

These dogs were used
in war. They helped their
owners fight enemies.

They also **guarded** land.
The big dogs scared outsiders.

People prized the breed's strength.
They watched mastiffs battle.

In 1835, England banned
mastiff fights.

People **bred** mastiffs to be gentle.

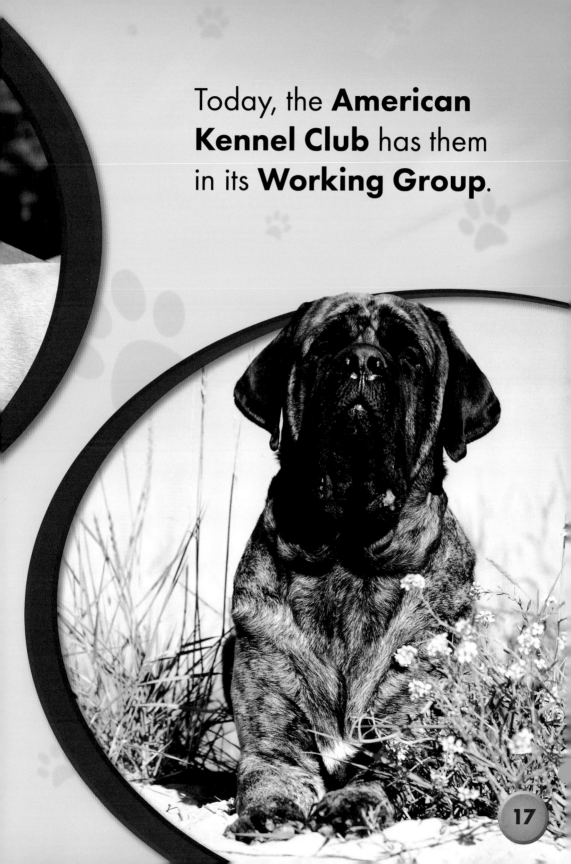

Today, the **American Kennel Club** has them in its **Working Group**.

17

Loyal and Loving

Mastiffs are still great guard dogs.
They bark loudly at strangers.

But mastiffs are quiet and lazy around people they know.

Mastiffs like to be near their families. They are good with children and other pets.

These **loyal** dogs will follow
their owners anywhere!

Glossary

American Kennel Club—an organization that keeps track of dog breeds in the United States

bred—purposely mating two dogs to make puppies with certain qualities

breed—a type of dog

brindle—a solid coat color mixed with streaks or spots of another color

fawn—a light brown color

guarded—kept safe

loyal—having constant support for someone

masks—patterns of dark color around the eyes, noses, and mouths of mastiffs

Working Group—a group of dog breeds that have a history of performing jobs for people

wrinkles—lines of skin or fur

To Learn More

AT THE LIBRARY

Bluemel Oldfield, Dawn. *English Mastiff: The World's Heaviest Dog*. New York, N.Y.: Bearport Publishing, 2013.

Bowman, Chris. *Great Danes*. Minneapolis, Minn.: Bellwether Media, 2016.

Morey, Allan. *Mastiffs*. North Mankato, Minn.: Capstone Press, 2016.

ON THE WEB

Learning more about mastiffs is as easy as 1, 2, 3.

1. Go to www.factsurfer.com.

2. Enter "mastiffs" into the search box.

3. Click the "Surf" button and you will see a list of related web sites.

With factsurfer.com, finding more information is just a click away.

Index

The images in this book are reproduced through the courtesy of: cynoclub, front cover; Kachalkina Veronika, pp. 4-5; Jagodka, p. 5; Photology1971, p. 6; Lerche&Johnson, p. 7; Tierfotoagentur/ Alamy, pp. 8-9, 14-15, 16-17, 17; Susan Schmitz, p. 9 (left, right); rokopix, pp. 10-11; Ricantimages, pp. 11, 18-19; Douglas Miller/ Getty, p. 12; Claudio Gennari, p. 13; Waldemar Dabrowski, p. 15; Maiorescu Mihaela, p. 19; Jaromir Chalabala, pp. 20-21; Newspix/ Getty, p. 21.